RESET YOUR GOALS
Jos Andrews

*Thank you to the nine special people
here – from old friends to new!*

Thank you also Sir G!

*And thanks to everyone who has been involved
in the publication of this book.*

J.A

Published by Rily Publications Ltd 2019
ISBN 978-1-84967-4065
Copyright © Jos Andrews 2019
The rights of Jos Andrews to be identified as the author
of this work has been asserted by her in accordance with
the Copyright, Designs and Patents Act 1988.

The Quick Reads project in Wales is an initiative coordinated by the
Welsh Books Council and supported by the Welsh Government.

The author and publisher would like to thank Welsh
Athletics for supplying the photo image of Lynn Davies
and for all of their support in writing this book.

Printed and bound by CPI Group (UK) Ltd, Croydon, CR0 4YY
Cover design by Welsh Books Council
Cover images SportingWales, Allstar

**CYNGOR LLYFRAU CYMRU
WELSH BOOKS COUNCIL**

Noddir gan
Lywodraeth Cymru
Sponsored by
Welsh Government

RESET YOUR GOALS

Jos Andrews

Don't worry about failures – worry about the chances you miss when you don't even try. In this book, sportsmen and women talk honestly about dealing with success and disappointment, and the common message is, 'I might get knocked down but I get up again. Setbacks are challenges but they don't defeat me.' In the words of Wales' Olympic gold medallist:

'If it's to be, it's up to me.'

Lynn Davies (featured)

Chapters

Foreword

Wales has always had a proud tradition of sporting excellence. Year after year, Welsh sportsmen and women continue to excite and inspire in sporting arenas all over the world. How does this come about? The stories in this book outline some of the background, the dedication and the sheer determination of these special people to succeed, sometimes against all the odds, in order to achieve sporting excellence.

The road to the top is never easy and even when great things are achieved, they can be cruelly snatched away by injury, unforeseen circumstances or just pure bad luck. This book is as much about highly talented individuals coming to terms with disappointment as coping with success. Each one has had to reset their goals.

C'mon, Wales!

CHAPTER ONE
Colin Jackson CBE

Athlete. Olympic, World, European and Commonwealth
Games medallist. Four times world record holder.

I've had a great life. I was very fortunate to have loving
parents and a wonderful sister, plus teachers and coaches,
who all encouraged me in my ambitions, as well as friends
who have been there for me in good and bad times. Added
to this I had a single-minded determination to succeed in
all that I did. It took time and great effort, but the results
were well worth it. It didn't come easily every time, but
never once did I think of giving up.

You've got to believe in what you do. You can't get away
with pretending. You have to be honest with yourself and
not try to kid yourself if you haven't prepared properly.
From the age of seventeen I dedicated everything to
hurdling. In sport, it was easy to see those who weren't
in shape because they hadn't done the work, and they
tried to make excuses. Honesty and integrity are crucial
because you'll get found out quickly if you don't have
these qualities.

Failure for me carries a sense of achievement almost
as much as success. Learning to fail is one of the most
important lessons to learn. You become resilient through

failure because you learn to find a way for it not to happen again. Every failure gives you an opportunity to learn more about yourself. It prepares you for handling future pitfalls in your life. It didn't matter if I hadn't done well in a race or wasn't able to nail a dance on *Strictly Come Dancing*; the feeling I had was the same. You have to learn to deal with the emotion, put it aside and try again.

Failure is a way of teaching you how to build towards success. It helps you appreciate success so much more. You learn to control the things that you *can* control. For me, that was taking responsibility for my training. If I had done my best, then that was the best I could do. When you succeed through your own efforts, the feeling is sweet. I won world titles and broke world records and, on the way, learnt to deal with failure as well as enjoying the good times.

Hard work at the right times, and on the right things, matters. Trying hard consistently is very important. My coach, Malcolm Arnold, would always remind me to keep my eye on the real goal and not be distracted on the way. I used to love weightlifting and I'd try to set myself bigger weights in the gym. He'd say, 'What for? Because it looks good?' He would remind me: 'You're not a weightlifter. You lift weights to help you run fast, so I don't need you to focus on weightlifting. Stick to your ultimate goal.' It was a good lesson. You have to focus on what is relevant. These lessons are from years ago, but I still apply them today.

I often get asked, 'Can you remember times when you failed?' Absolutely! The question you have to ask yourself is, 'Why did you fail?' The reason can sometimes be very obvious, sometimes not. As an athlete if I didn't do well in a training session, the answer might be because I was tired. It's the next question that's important: 'Why were you tired?' Sometimes you have to check that you're not using excuses. It's important to think about the consequences of your actions and not just settle for failure. You have to learn to ask yourself the real reasons for failure and not just make up excuses to justify it.

Years ago, I was constantly battling against the great Roger Kingdom in my races. We were jostling for the world number one position and were one all when we went to Nice in France. I led him all the way, came off the final hurdle as clear leader and suddenly caught my foot on the floor, staggered, and Roger just drifted past me and took the victory! He became world number one and I was furious that I'd led all the way through the early, hard parts of the race but at the end, which should have been the easy part, I'd switched off and he'd won. Three days later I had to race him again in Crystal Palace, and in my mind I felt I should have been two ahead at this point, not trying to equal him. I roared out of the blocks and hammered ahead and won. I kept thinking I should have been three ahead but instead we were equal at two all. In the next race Roger broke the world record. It was a bitter blow but, in the end, it gave me the motivation to break that record. My world record time outdoors stood for many years after that, but I learnt never to dwell on success but to move on to the next competition. Winning gives you motivation but it's not the end. The key when you've achieved something is to set yourself your next target and focus on that.

We all know how hard it is to feel that things have been unfair. When you've put in the time and effort and things don't turn out as you thought they would, it's tough. But you've got to be gracious in defeat to be a true champion. It's easy to look at people and see the successes they have but things aren't always as they seem. People on the outside only see the good times, only see success. You crossed the line first, you won the game, now you have the flash car and big house. People have to remember what it has taken to achieve that. These things don't come on a plate. It's down to all the time you put in when it's cold or it's wet. It's about the things you gave up, like friends' parties, Christmas dinner and late nights out with your mates. You have to balance what you want against what you have to do or to give up to get there.

When I was seventh in the Olympic Games in Barcelona in 1992, I had been pre-race favourite for the gold medal.

But my training partner and great friend Mark McCoy won. I felt devastated. To lose when the eyes of the world were on me and then to suffer horrendous comments and criticisms in the press was very hard to take. But I had to face up to that bitter defeat and move on. You have to learn to fail in your life. It's hard but you have to. It's a message I always try to share with people. Hold your head up high and move on. Don't just sit there, dwelling on what has happened to you. Come out again and refocus for another day. Take control. Set yourself a new target, a new goal, a new competition to aim for. It might be that you didn't get the job you'd set your heart on or you didn't achieve the exam results you wanted. Whatever you did and didn't get, take time to ask yourself the reasons why and then move on.

Allen Johnson, one of the best high hurdlers of all time, who went on to be the world and Olympic champion, was going to race me for the first time in Edinburgh. He got out of the blocks so swiftly that I can remember thinking, 'Who is this?' But all of a sudden he was no longer there, and I crossed the line as the clear winner. He tells the story that he got to hurdle eight and said to himself, 'I'm running against the champion Colin Jackson,' and as soon as he thought that – crash – he was lost! By focusing on me as his rival competitor, instead of on himself and his race, he lost. It's a good reminder of how important it is to keep your mind on your own goal. Don't waste time thinking about what others are doing. My way of dealing with it would have been to think, 'This is MY race' and I would smile. If I lost, I would be thinking, 'Next time, the race will be mine.' My thought was always, 'Go for it,' not just, 'Give it a go.' I wouldn't think about defeat ahead of a race, though it's never good to be overconfident and cocky either, because you won't keep your mind on what you need to do.

You've always got to keep reassessing your goals and not settle. Even after gaining twenty-five major championship medals and breaking four world records, one of which is still standing now, I could never be content to stay as I was. Spending time making small adjustments will all add up to an overall improvement. Never be satisfied. Keep testing yourself. Good questions to ask yourself might be: Were you really prepared? Had you done the work? Were you the right fit for this? If you'd honestly done all you could do, then move on and look to the next target. Stick with it and eventually your hard work will pay off. Believe in yourself and the work that you've done.

When an athlete retires from sport, they discover their true value and worth. It's a time when they're at their most vulnerable because they're no longer the best at their chosen sport. You have to know yourself and believe in yourself and your capabilities. You can't hide behind a title or brand anymore, you have to almost reinvent yourself and build your own new brand – you. I did question what was I going to do with the rest of my life. When you're so used to a rigid training and competing regime it's very difficult to change. Up until then, my life had been very organised and mapped out. I could tell you where I was going to be, week after week. Now it was going to be very different, so I had to give serious thought to what I wanted to do and how I should go about doing it. I didn't panic because I felt that some of the skills I'd learnt to prepare for my sport would also help me as I thought about a new career. In order to succeed now, I had to learn new skills and play to my strengths. This is when you learn to appreciate what you have. Be true to yourself. Question yourself and never be afraid of the answer.

My new career path after athletics surprised even me! Little did I know that in a few short years I would be broadcasting from the Olympic Games, diving with sharks for a television programme, cooking in a studio kitchen for *Masterchef* and learning brand-new skills on the dance floor in *Strictly Come Dancing*. Although this was very new territory for me, I was determined to do my best and applied sports techniques to help me. I listened and learnt along the way. I've made great friends across the world of sport and they all say that my determination marks me out in everything I do.

In life the only time you get defeated is when you give up, not when somebody defeats you. When you stop trying, that's when it's over!

CHAPTER TWO
Mica Moore

Athlete. Team Wales Commonwealth Games.
Bobsleigh. Team GB Winter Olympic Games.

My parents were good at sport; my dad had a rugby background and my mum did sprinting when she was younger. Both of them were always in the gym and they took me with them. I've tried every sport and that's good. Anyone can take part at whatever level they choose. You set your own goals and work within that.

I started sprinting relatively late when I was about fifteen years old and settled on athletics. I'd been going to a youth club and spending lots of time with my friends before my parents took me to Newport Harriers and said I should do athletics seriously – and I loved it! I made so many new friends and really enjoyed the training. There aren't many people who say they enjoy training, but I loved it. I like keeping fit and I enjoy the discipline of training. I found that I was quite good at sprinting and in my first year I competed for Wales in the Celtic Games. I was a really young member of the team and, having enjoyed the experience, made my mind up to try to be selected for the Commonwealth Games in Glasgow in 2014.

I had a few coaches, but eventually my dad became

my coach. I sat down with him and told him my goal. We worked on that together. Dad and I are quite similar and have the perfect blend of personalities. He is very laid-back, but he sets the goals and I take them on. We've never had an argument or fallen out in training. If ever it gets heated in training, it's because I'm cross with myself and my performance and he understands that because he is a sportsman himself and knows what those emotions feel like. There's not really anybody else I would trust with my sporting ambitions other than my dad. I feel comfortable being able to talk through my targets with him. He knows when I'm tired, when I need a longer rest or even when I need to put in more training. He'll be honest with me and say, 'I don't think you should do that race yet. I think you need a few more weeks.'

As it happened, I wasn't picked to go as an individual athlete to the Commonwealth Games but as part of the 4 x 100 relay team. Winning a Welsh vest brought home to me how proud I was to be Welsh. There aren't too many occasions where you can compete for Wales so this meant the world to me. The Olympics is obviously a pinnacle in anyone's career but the Commonwealth Games gave me the chance to wear the red vest proudly. It is just such an honour to compete for Wales. We are a small country and to be able to put it on the map in sport is very important.

I'm always very hard on myself and I had to pinch

myself before I realised that I would be part of the team. Even when coach Scott Simpson rang to tell me that I'd been selected, I couldn't believe it. My dad always says to me, 'Focus on the processes, the outcomes will take care of themselves.' That is great advice and I still concentrate on what I need to do to reach my goal, not what the final outcome might be.

Being an only child helps you focus on your own path in life. I'm not used to having people around me all the time but being part of a relay team was good. Having the support of others around me was really helpful and contributed a great deal to our success.

There were a lot of training camps before the Commonwealth Games. The squad began with eight of us which was then whittled down to six and we were expected to be at all of the intensive camps. We were close friends, trained hard together and that really helped us look out for one another. Maybe we weren't as quick as the other teams, but we had a very strong bond. Any feedback we gave each other was positive and supportive, aimed at helping one another and strengthening our togetherness as a team.

My aim was not only to go out there and perform to the best of my ability, but also to enjoy it and to take in the experience. Being at a home Games helped too, as my family were able to be there to support me. The crowd were fantastic in their response to the home nations. We were one of the youngest teams, so not much was expected of us, but we still put pressure on ourselves to show what we could do. We had a little mishap in the heat and then an anxious wait to find out if we had qualified for the final, but we made it! Unfortunately, we didn't win any medals, but all the team's effort and hard work was worth it.

After the Games, my athletics training continued, and I went to a warm-weather camp in Arizona. In the middle of doing a session there, I suddenly felt terrible. I had been running well and I thought, 'I can't wait to compete again,' but during the session I became out of breath and my technique got worse. I couldn't work out what was going wrong. I had come down with a virus. I wasn't sure what it was or where it came from, but it hit me very hard and wiped out my whole athletics season and into the next year. I felt as if I could hardly move. I couldn't run a hundred metres, which is devastating for a sprinter. I would run thirty metres and suddenly get terrible cramps and spasms all over my body.

It was such a shame as things had been going so well for me. Maybe it was my body saying that I needed a break. I was very upset and I'm not a person who usually is like that. I'm generally a very happy person, but it hit me hard. I'd begin training and try my best, but my body just wouldn't work as it had. It was a very long process and the doctors were unable to find out exactly what was wrong with me. Sport is my love and if you're unable to do what you love it's frustrating and also deeply upsetting. It's easy to get disheartened and I'm thankful that I had such a good support system around me with family, friends and coaches. My mum and dad were always there for me, but it was a tough time. In athletics you have short seasons, small windows of opportunity to compete and I felt helpless, seeing everyone else being able to do what I couldn't. To watch other athletes going off to the Welsh Championships and the British Trials and performing well was really difficult. Dad encouraged me constantly not to give up and his phrase which kept me going was 'Stick at it. Stick at it and it'll come back.'

I was very upset at not being able to continue my athletics and felt very down. Luckily, I had a friend in the bobsleigh team and he suggested that I go along for some trials to see how I got on. He pointed out that because of my illness I was a little bit heavier and even if I couldn't run as far, I still had good core strength and would be perfect for the bobsleigh. This opportunity was appealing because it allowed me to shift my goals and gave me a chance to motivate myself again. My new training regime was like athletics – sprinting, lifting similar weights and doing gym sessions. This got me through those dark times. The support of those around me was positive, too.

I spoke to a sports psychologist who helped me so much by changing the way I looked at things. She taught me how to change my goals, and my mindset, and to focus on other things instead.

I went to the bobsleigh trials in Birmingham with my dad who told me to give it a go, and just see what happened. I had to do a 60m sprint, and then push a rollbob, a bobsleigh on wheels. It all went really well. After several more tests and trials I qualified for the Winter Olympics in South Korea! I could hardly believe it! I knew very little really about bobsleigh but in a way that worked for me. If I had known everything I know now, I think I would've been quite scared! Bobsleigh is harsh, tough and can be cruel and unforgiving. You might ask: why am I doing it? Well, because I absolutely love my job as the brake woman! It's all about applying that force, to get speed and power to the sled. Sometimes you crash, or your race doesn't go well, or the time isn't what you wanted, even though you've given it everything. But all of that is forgotten, as you strive towards the one competition that every athlete dreams about – the Olympic Games!

In my first year of bobsleigh, my driver and I had an incredible season and we became world junior champions, finishing the season on a high. But two weeks before we were due to start the next season, we were called into a meeting to be told that our funding was going to be cut and they would be funding the men instead. We were shattered by the decision but decided that we wouldn't be beaten by that bombshell. We set up a crowdfunding page, contacted the media to share the story and, within six days, we had raised £30,000, the minimum we needed – a fantastic achievement!

I'm the brake woman at the back of the sled. Another Mica (yes, we've both got the same name) is the driver at the front. At the start, we both push together and hit the sled off the top and she'll get in after about thirty metres and I'll continue pushing for another twenty to thirty-five metres, then I'll get in at the back and she'll drive down the track. I'll be as still as possible and then brake at the end. At first, I found it really scary! My dad and my boyfriend were at the end of a phone before a race just calming my nerves. Once you're in the sled, you're in, and there's no escape! You've just got to do the things you practise. We have to put our trust in each other. As I learnt in Glasgow, being part of a team is everything.

Dad was still my primary coach and he would plan and supervise the majority of my training, but I also had an ice coach and Mica had a driving coach. Mica and I set a goal of a top-ten finish, thinking that could be achievable, but we didn't tell anybody. We'd never been to the Olympic track and didn't really know what to expect. We set tough training goals to help us feel confident going into the Games.

I felt lucky that I'd been to the Commonwealth Games earlier as it prepared me for competing at the highest level, but the Olympic Games was on an entirely different scale! We tried to show each other that we were comfortable and calm. It was important to remember that Mica as the driver was taking us down a track at eighty to ninety miles per hour, so I had to make sure she had a clear head and wasn't thinking about all those turns. I wanted her to have complete confidence in me and I'm sure she felt the same.

Mica had never driven the track before, which could have been nerve-wracking, but we flipped that and saw it as a positive, in that we had a blank page to work on. That really suited us. The way that the start was set up was perfect for me as it was very similar to the one at Bath where we trained at home. I told myself, 'I've run this track a billion times and I know how to run it, that's all I need to do!' On the day of the race we switched off our phones and all contact on social media. We just chilled, ate and listened to music. I'm so glad we did because although in bobsleigh, like sprinting, the margins between success and failure are very small, we didn't want to know where we stood in the race but rather have clear minds to compete without any external pressure. I haven't watched any recordings of the Games; all I have are wonderful memories of a fantastic experience. We were thrilled with what we achieved. We finished in eighth position, the best ever by a British women's Olympic bobsleigh team.

That was my last bobsleigh race. I haven't raced since the Olympics and, in a way, I'm glad I haven't. It was the most incredible experience. I really liked the fact that in bobsleigh everyone was so friendly. There's almost a union of brake women and drivers. Lolo Jones, the great American hurdler, was one of my heroes who I used to watch on television. She is now competing in bobsleigh and I couldn't believe that someone of that standing would come over and talk to me. 'Hi, we're brake women, how are you feeling about this?' It was almost surreal! I texted my cousin to say, 'Lolo Jones just talked to me!!!' You make great connections and you realise that maybe we're all the same with the same fears and worries. Teams help each other as much as they can. If someone's helmet is broken, it's: 'Borrow mine!' It's such an extreme sport that everyone tries to support and comfort everyone else. I think I've made a lot of lifelong friends from bobsleigh.

I'm now studying for a Master's degree in Sports Broadcasting at Cardiff Met University, knowing that if I want to I can return to bobsleigh. I'm very happy with what I have achieved and I'm looking forward now to the next phases of my career. I understand the importance of having other strands to my life. This course is my next goal, though I'd love to achieve more in athletics. I like to challenge myself in all I do. I've tried boxing and I might try rugby, who knows? There are very few times in my life that I've thought 'I don't enjoy this anymore.' When I was ill, it was difficult to see how I would ever come back, but I'm so glad that I got through it, and Dad was right – you just have to stick it out. There will be a time when it comes right, and things fall into place.

I listen to motivational videos if I'm struggling, and one message that stands out for me that I listened to before bobsleigh runs was 'How bad do you want it?' The message was that when you want to succeed as badly as you want to breathe, then you'll be successful! I have inspirational quotes tattooed on me and the one that helped me through bobsleigh was 'only the fearless can be great'. In bobsleigh you're bound to be fearful but as I kept telling myself in the build-up to the Games, 'Grab this opportunity – you're going to be very scared at times but just get through it and it will be well worth it!'

It certainly was!

CHAPTER THREE
Simon Jones MBE

Cricketer. Glamorgan, Worcestershire,
Hampshire and England.

It's a weird feeling playing for England as a Welshman. The annoying thing is that people don't understand it – it's the England and Wales Cricket Board. I'm a very proud Welshman, proud to be good enough to have played in an England side.

As a youngster I was naturally talented at a range of sports. But I was more interested in football than anything else and had trials for Leeds. I was a very small boy, but had grown quickly by the age of fifteen. My father, Jeff Jones, an international cricketer himself, wasn't at all pushy but encouraged and backed me. There was pressure from others as 'Son of Jeff' but never from him. One of the best things is that we are part of a father and son special group who have played for England. I think there are only fourteen in the history of the game!

I was lucky also in that I had great teachers who encouraged me. In primary school, Eifion Thomas, my headmaster, loved sport and helped me enormously, and in my secondary school, Coedcae Comprehensive, another fantastic teacher, John Prickett, was an inspiration. I won a scholarship to Millfield, a school which has produced a number of talented sportsmen and women. I had two years there working with top class coaches and making wonderful friends who I still keep in contact with to this day.

I turned professional when I was sixteen and still at school. Matthew Maynard, the Glamorgan captain at the time, came down to Millfield School to see me, watched me in the nets and signed me up there and then. I was hugely proud – it was a dream come true! Very importantly, it meant that I would be following in my father's footsteps. There was no pressure for me to do that, but I wanted to, and I wanted to represent England like him as well – two fast bowlers from the same family!

It was a tough start to go straight from school to becoming a professional. It was a massive step. And it was hard to be surrounded by adults – I'd been taught by my parents to respect my elders so I didn't really speak much in the changing room. I often used to get ribbed about it, but I had been brought up only to speak when you're spoken to. It's very different today, I know!

The biggest turning point in my career was when I went to Australia with Rodney Marsh, the famous Australian wicket-keeper, and the England Academy in 2001 – I came back a different young man. Rod was amazing with me – my father couldn't get over the difference! I had changed not only physically, but also as a person. I was more confident, and I'd have a go at anything. I had been painfully shy, so overcoming this was a huge achievement. To be where I am now, doing after-dinner speaking and question and answer sessions, is amazing. I have also done work for Sky TV and recently I was invited by the WRU to speak to the Welsh rugby team before the Wales v Australia game as someone who has had success against the Australians. It was a huge honour; growing up I would never have imagined being able to do that.

I was still living with my parents when I had a phone call from the chief of selectors, David Graveney, telling me I had been chosen to play for England. I'd been waiting and waiting, hoping I might get the call, and this was it. I was bouncing. It's what you dream of, isn't it? To play at Lords on my debut against India, against Sachin Tendulkar and those guys, was incredible. I'd never played at Lords so that would be an experience in itself.

I remember walking into the changing room and I was a bit late because I'd had to catch the train up to London, as I wasn't driving at the time. Everyone was in their place and it was very intimidating to walk into the England dressing room for the first time and see all those star cricketers. I was thinking, 'Where am I going to sit? What do I do? Do I just stand here like a lemon?' The most experienced and the most successful guy in that changing room, Alec Stewart, then moved his stuff saying, 'Come and sit by me.' I knew I was all right then. He regretted it later because of the mess I made! He was ridiculously tidy and regimented in his ways and I'm quite the opposite ... but I will never forget his gesture. Him moving his stuff and letting me sit down put me at ease straight away.

To go in the changing room and sit next to Alec Stewart and men like him who I'd seen on TV was a lot to take in. It doesn't get better than that. You learn so much being in touching distance of your England teammates. You can get to know people very quickly in those situations. I was fortunate in that a lot of those guys, although very successful, were also really down to earth and set a good example to a new young team member like me.

As a cricketer, playing for England is a big thing – there's more money and there's more recognition. A lot can happen to you very quickly. The important thing is to be yourself. Don't try to change; don't get ahead of yourself.

For that debut game we were lucky because we batted first, so I had a couple of days just to let everything soak in. When, finally, I walked out to bowl, I couldn't feel my legs because I was so nervous. There's a picture of me with my arm around Nasser Hussain and I was telling him, 'Nasser, I can't feel my legs.' He said, 'I can help you get out there, but I can't help you bowl!' As soon as I got the first one or two balls down and they'd gone more or less where I wanted them to, I was alright. My dad was in the crowd and I could see him clearly. Every time I walked back to my mark, I had a little look up at him and he gave me a thumbs up. It was like being in a dream. I kept looking around, thinking, 'Am I actually here? Am I bowling to Sachin Tendulkar, Virender Sehwag and V.V.S. Laxman, batting legends of the game? With Alec Stewart keeping wicket and Graham Thorpe and guys like that in the slips?' It was surreal.

I suppose two of the great highlights of my international career were against Australia, but for very different reasons. In 2002, whilst fielding on the boundary in the First Test in Brisbane and sliding to field a ball, I ruptured an anterior cruciate ligament in my knee. I knew how badly injured I was from the sheer pain. I wouldn't let anyone touch me. The Aussie crowd gave me a hard time and I know that they were there as paying spectators and felt they had a right to say what they wanted. But you can't condone some of the awful things they said. To be called a 'weak, Pommie bastard' when I was being carried off on a stretcher I thought was more than a bit cruel. Someone also threw a can of beer at me. I don't think he realised when he threw it that because of that injury my tour was over. I was going home and wouldn't play for eighteen months. My dream of playing in the Ashes had been shattered.

To think that my career was over was awful. But I was fortunate enough to have a very good friend who was a physio at Glamorgan and he encouraged me, saying he'd get me back to full fitness. I kept positive people around me. It was a long rehabilitation, undergoing exercises for five hours a day, six days a week for eighteen months. If you want to achieve anything in life you have to put the hard yards in. There's no cutting corners, because that's when things go wrong. I did everything I was asked to and worked as hard as I could.

I returned to the England Academy in 2003 and went to India with Rod Marsh. I felt strong and fit and I was bowling fast again. Then Rod pulled me out of one session to tell me I was going to be part of the Test team to the West Indies! I couldn't believe it! I'd had a taste of international cricket and I wanted it back ... badly! This was the reward for all the graft and the sacrifices I'd made. I didn't drink for a year and a half because I didn't want anything to hamper my recovery. I knew when I would be ready and now I was ready to go.

Following a very successful tour of the West Indies and more Tests against other international sides, I was chosen again to play against Australia in 2005, but this time at home. This was going to be an Ashes series that would stay in the memory for a very long time. As a fast bowler, I desperately wanted to show that after battling back from injury, I could compete with the very best. We were a young England side up against players who were, even then, cricketing legends. I got lots of wickets in the third Test and in the first innings of the fourth Test, but in the second innings, injury struck again.

I actually got the injury in the first Test. Obviously we didn't let the press know because we didn't want the Aussies to know I was struggling. But I pulled out of the second innings of the fourth Test because I'd tried to get up that morning and I couldn't walk; I couldn't put my foot on the ground. I was sent to rehab to try to get fit for the last Test in the Oval, but it was no good. I had three or four bone spurs floating in my ankle and one had cracked off. This was to be my last international appearance.

Several of my teammates in that Ashes series have gone on to do other things. Andrew Strauss became Director of England Cricket, while Freddie Flintoff, Kevin Pieterson and Michael Vaughan do media work. When they were thinking about what they were going to do next, I was still focused on trying to get fit again. I missed out on a lot of opportunities which I should have taken, but I turned them down because of the state of mind I was in. It wouldn't have been fair on the people asking me to work for them because I wouldn't have been able to do myself justice. I couldn't change anything; that's life, and things happen for a reason.

The next year, I took my parents to meet the Queen when I collected my MBE and that was very special. I was also named Wisden Cricketer of the Year and my dad was there to see it. To be chosen as one of the top five in the year was a fantastic achievement and something I'm very proud of. To be acknowledged alongside the legends of the game, the people you admire, is humbling. It doesn't sink in when your heroes, people you look up to, like Matthew Hoggard, Steve Harmison and Freddie Flintoff, congratulate you on being a good bowler. To know you're rated and valued by the best is very special. Dad felt proud, but sad too, that both of our careers had been blighted by injury. Both of us understood the frustration and pain of going through this. Throughout it all, Dad was always there for me.

You get days when you're down, when you think, 'What the hell am I doing?' That's why it's so important to keep good people around you who'll say, 'Right, snap out of it. We're doing this today, so get on with it.' You don't want to take the easy option of giving up. It's a slippery slope. The little niggling demons are always there in your head, making you think about what you could be doing, not what you *are* doing. Talking to family and good friends who wanted the best for me kept me on the straight and narrow.

I carried on playing at county level for Glamorgan,

Worcestershire and Hampshire but wasn't really able to bowl as I had done, because of injury. It was inevitable really that I'd have to give up playing the game I loved. I turned to coaching, starting my own academy, and I'm thoroughly enjoying being part of the development of future cricketers. I really enjoy coaching young people. You have to make it fun and relevant to them. There are challenges in building my academy, but I want to pass on my skills. I want to be part of bringing on the next generation of Welsh fast bowlers and batters. It'll take time, but I want it to be done properly. I want to give them the attention they need. You work hard at the areas that you're weak on. You don't just work on the things you enjoy doing. And you certainly don't just do the things you're good at. You have to have an attitude that spurs you to want to become better and to be the best you can be, whether in your fitness, fielding, batting or bowling. Sometimes you have to take a good look at yourself and realise that life can be tough if you want to get to where you want to be.

Cricket is an exceptionally tough sport because it's so multidimensional. There are so many aspects of the game that can affect your performance. If you want to be good at anything you have to graft, and you have to listen, and that's when you start to become better and enjoy what you do.

If you're at the receiving end of 'sledging', being intimidated or verbally insulted, my advice would be to ignore it. Don't get involved. Those who try to put you off by saying how good they are, and how well they're going to play or how bad you are often get caught out. The best thing is to say nothing and let your game do the talking. As you get older you can deal with it a lot better and there were times when I found it quite good fun.

You have to be a good people manager when you're coaching. Some people need a stick, others need a carrot to encourage them. I responded to the carrot, whereas some of the lads I played alongside needed a stick. It's important that you understand and adapt to people; what you don't want to do is put them off the game. You have to build confidence in young people. If they don't believe in themselves, no one will. I try to get children to back themselves and have a go. It's important to keep on trying and know that you will get better. Attitude is so important. You can have all the ability in the world but if you're lazy, you'll get caught out. Staying grounded and being humble and respectful are the three things I stick by. If you don't, you'll struggle. It's important also not to expect things to come easily. You have to learn to be resilient and take the rough with the smooth and look at the big picture. Enjoy it while you can. If you get an opportunity, grab it with both hands. Never take things for granted.

My heroes were every single person I played with in that 2005 Ashes side. There was so much pride for each other in that England dressing room. I also respect Shane Warne, Brian Lara and Sachin Tendulkar as greats of the game. 'Great' is used far too easily but they were truly wonderful players who gave up their time to help others and remained very humble throughout.

My dad always said to me, 'You'll have bad days. You'll have a lot of them – just remember to think of the good days. Tomorrow is another day. Always remain positive.'

CHAPTER FOUR

Professor Laura McAllister CBE

Football player. Millwall Lionesses, Cardiff City, Wales.

I grew up in a sports-mad home in Bridgend with a mum and dad who were both sportspeople, but ironically football was probably the least popular sport in our house. However, my cousins and friends all played football and the boys in my local village played football so I always seemed to end up kicking a ball around with them. They treated me as an equal and no quarter was given – and that was fine by me! I could play football and I never felt any discrimination or prejudice because they knew I was as good a footballer as they were!

All that was okay until I went to Bryntirion Comprehensive School in Bridgend. In Ysgol Glyndŵr Junior School I was still able to play in teams in the playground, but in secondary school when sport became more structured and formal there wasn't an opportunity to play with boys as the PE classes were strictly divided into boys and girls. It was rugby and football for the boys and netball and hockey for the girls. I played every sport, but football was the game I most wanted to play. Thinking back, I didn't want to stand out and be seen as different, but I remember feeling that this was wrong, that there weren't the same chances for me. I couldn't play in the school team where some of the boys I'd grown up with, and who weren't as good as me, were playing every week. I can remember feeling indignant, disappointed and cross, and speaking to my PE teachers about it, saying, 'This isn't fair.' That was what really bothered me – the lack of fairness. I didn't feel that I should have something that other children didn't have; I felt that others were having something I couldn't have, just because I was a girl.

It was a good lesson for me, learning to be confident about my rights and what people are entitled to – in my case fair play. I just wanted the right to have the same chance, irrespective of gender, to play the game I loved and that I was good at. It taught me the importance of speaking up and made me understand the need to use my voice against inequality. It's important not to be frightened by authority, because actually I had a very good response from my teachers when I made my feelings known. My PE teachers, Beverley Pearce, Cynthia Morgan and Barbara Owens were Welsh hockey Internationals themselves and they understood that girls could do as well as boys in sport. They were supportive and gave me opportunities to play football alongside netball and hockey. I think they respected the fact that I had spoken my mind about how I felt in a clear and honest way. It's a good lesson for all young people to learn to say how they feel, but not in a rude or aggressive manner. As long as you do it respectfully and politely, the chances are people will listen and respond favourably.

By making clear what I wanted, I went on to play for Cardiff City and Wales. If you had said that to the six-year-old me, pretending to lift the FA cup in the mirror in my bedroom, I'd never have believed I would achieve what I did – playing for Cardiff City, playing in the Premier League, winning 24 caps for my country and, most of all, captaining Wales. These are dreams that you can never imagine coming true, but they did because girls and women before me spoke up. They raised these issues with the Football Association of Wales to make sure that we girls had the same rights, and for that I am grateful. Without it we'd never have got to a position where these days it is entirely accepted that girls can play football.

When I went to university, I played for Millwall Lionesses who were one of the big teams of the time. They were a really good side and I was building my fitness up, so I valued every game I was picked for. When I returned home, I joined Cardiff City which was great because it was properly structured football. At the time, there was never any certainty elsewhere that we would be able to play football correctly, with linesmen, referees, goal posts, nets and matching kit. Things have moved on now, thankfully, but I remember those times very clearly. Everything that the club had done, they had done themselves. They had set up in 1975 as a group of women who organised themselves professionally to achieve their aims. I felt very proud to be playing for them because they were a football club, just like any men's club.

I feel strongly that nothing lands in your lap. You have to take on responsibility. Any good sportsperson will tell you that what makes them hungry for success is that they have had to work hard for it. There is danger if things come too easily. Sport is about a physical and mental desire to be the best you can be, and having things too easily isn't good. You have to know what hard work looks like to enjoy the experience of doing well. You have to put the effort in yourself. Like everything, there's no point in turning up if you aren't prepared, ready to give your best and to maintain high standards. Don't be late, and be respectful to all those who are helping you, most of whom will be giving up their time voluntarily to coach and officiate. In return, you have every right to expect good standards from those working with you. It's important that respect is two-way.

It's easy to name your sporting heroes across all sports, but what about those unsung heroes who devote their lives to young men and women who don't reach the highest standards, but only want to participate in and enjoy their chosen sport? My role models are also those closer to home, like my PE teachers at school. They didn't believe that sport was only for those who were good at it. They appreciated that all girls could have fun playing. You don't have to be good at sport to enjoy it. Other role models were women like Karen Jones and Michele Adams who ran the club at Cardiff City. They were great players and also good coaches and officials who rolled up their sleeves and worked hard to make the club function well and I really admired that dedication. They ran a team at the top level but also built for the future, working with the under twelves, under sixteens and other junior teams. For these people, who so often do this for nothing, there are no great glittering financial rewards, but they care about sport and are passionate in their commitment. They want to make the future better for girls who come after them. They really deserve the MBEs they were awarded.

There's a game or a sport out there for absolutely everyone. Whether you're very talented or simply having a go, what matters is that you enjoy it. Sport has given me so much in my life. It's made me more fit and healthy, more alert and energetic. Being active for life is just one aspect though. In striving to play the sport I love, I've learned how to deal with people and I've made many great friends. Sport has also taught me the importance of setting goals and being able to adapt and strive to achieve the best I can. I learnt to set high standards in sport and that has helped me set high standards for myself in my work too. It's good to have high ambitions. There's lots of things I've wanted to do and maybe haven't always achieved, but I don't regret trying. You have to be prepared to work to get the things you want. People look at the very best in sport, those at the top in football and rugby, for example, and think they like what comes with that position – money and fame – but they fail to realise that those people have to work very hard to maintain that position. To be the best, there are sacrifices to be made. To reach the top those sportsmen and women have to give up things that the rest of us take for granted, like late nights, parties and occasionally eating and drinking too much.

Every single moment of every day in life and work, I use the lessons I've learnt from sport. I think I've learnt more from sport than anything else I've done. Its skills and values have helped me be successful in other areas of my life. My confidence and my belief in myself have come from my sporting career. My ability to work in teams was learnt on playing fields. My trust in others and my ability to judge the character of others has been learnt this way too. And the ethics of sport are important – not cheating and fair play are great life lessons. You can say a lot about a person's character by the way they lose. If you cheat, you cheat yourself, first and foremost. If you win and you have done so honestly and fairly, it feels great!

CHAPTER FIVE
Matthew Jones

Football player. Leeds United, Leicester City and Wales.

My family weren't very sporty. My dad had a real passion for boxing but didn't really apply himself. My brother Neil was a decent footballer, but he joined the army.

I don't remember being told that I was good at sport in school but when I speak to friends and former teachers now, they tell me I always stood out. I didn't see that myself; I never thought I was good enough and that worked positively for me, because it made me try harder at everything. I always wanted to improve and I'm glad I had that attitude and that drive, because if I'd thought I was good, I might have become complacent. From a very young age I've always chased my dreams.

As children, my brother and I used to watch Bruce Lee and *Rocky* films with my dad on Friday nights and I was always inspired by them. My brother was two years older than me and the moment the film stopped, we'd go straight into a brawl in the middle of the living room. He'd always be more physical, because he was bigger and stronger than me and I had to find ways to take him on. The films motivated me as the underdog to challenge him – not that I always won!

I've never lost that need to have a go and try to challenge myself in different situations. I've always grasped opportunities when they came along. I began playing for Bwlch Rangers in Llanelli, playing football with my brother and other players older than me, training by kicking the ball against nearby garages. I then joined my local club, Seaside, which was a mile away from where I lived. My dad was too busy to drive me there, so for my first game I had to make my own way there and back. My challenge was to work out how long it would take me to run there and to be on time for the game. It taught me the importance of timekeeping and of learning how to manage myself. I had to make sure my boots were clean and that I had everything I needed in my kit. If I forgot anything, I had to miss the game because there was nobody to drive me back home! I'm glad, though, that I had to learn the hard way as it made me self-reliant and used to thinking problems out for myself.

After school, my parents were keen that I go outside to play so I'd call on best friends Jason Morris and Lee Davies, to try to persuade them to join me but they would usually be too busy playing on their electronic games. I'd then go outside dribbling the ball on my own, bouncing the ball on and off the kerb, smashing the ball against a neighbour's wall – and being moved on – or lobbing the ball against the side of a house and being chased off down the street. These long solo practice sessions really developed my technical ability.

A very special coach named Colin Thomas encouraged me to be organised. He taught me the very important and practical basics of football – to be on time, to have spare laces and to have polished boots. His constant message to the team was, 'By failing to prepare, you're preparing to fail.' It was a valuable lesson because later when my bootlaces snapped in an under 14 game, I had a spare pair to hand immediately. If I hadn't, I wouldn't have played in the game, I might not have gained my youth cap, and I might not have gone on to play for Wales! Someone else would have taken my place, grasped the opportunity and maybe shone in that game. I would have missed my chance because I hadn't been well prepared.

When I moved to Coedcae School, Llanelli, my friends were taken to school by car, but my parents insisted I make my own way there. I quickly realised that this, again, would teach me to be punctual. My grandfather had always told me, 'Five minutes early is always better than being on time or five minutes late.' It improved my fitness, too, because I set myself little challenges to get to certain places earlier than the day before, or to beat my friends who had lifts, but might be stuck at traffic lights. I set myself ridiculous targets, but little by little I could see that my speed, power, strength and agility was improving.

I never moaned about having to do this or saw it as being a negative. I took full responsibility for getting myself to school on time, even if usually I would dribble a ball all the way there! I couldn't wait to get home and then go out to play football in the street with my mates. I was called 'the engine' because I'd turn up on a Saturday and would be the fittest player there. I'd cover every blade of grass, trying to do my best at all times.

Soccer scouts came to watch me play at Seaside and I was nine years old when I was picked by Swansea Cygnets. I trained with them twice a week. A good friend of mine, Stuart Roberts, who also went on to play for Swansea, and his father Kelvin took me to practice and games. I always looked to Stuart to see if I could be as good as him. Kelvin also used to take us sometimes for training and I thank him for his help in improving my pace. Stuart and I, two Llanelli boys playing for Swansea, felt proud and were often thrilled with ourselves after a game – though we soon came down to earth, because coming back in the car Kelvin would remind us, 'You're only as good as your last game.' He never wanted us to get complacent and wanted us to understand that once the game was over, we needed to start preparing for the next week in order to be better.

Soon, I was approached by Oxford, Chelsea and a range of academy clubs. I went to Norwich, Liverpool and Coventry but then Glan Letheren, a former goalkeeper for Leeds (but who as it happened was originally from Llanelli), invited me to go to his old club. Every couple of weeks, at the age of twelve, I was travelling back and fore to Leeds on the train from Llanelli on my own, navigating all the changes of platforms. I loved it! Finally, I was invited at the age of fourteen to move to Leeds with two other players. It meant leaving my family, friends and school and living with people chosen to look after me. It meant missing Christmases and birthdays with the family. I was very homesick, but it gave me inner strength and it made me see that I'd have to make sacrifices and concentrate hard if I wanted to play top class football in the Premier League. I knew I'd have to give one hundred per cent to ensure that I wasn't giving up my life at home for nothing.

At the age of fifteen I was playing for the Leeds youth team, again with older boys. I made my first team debut two years later in the FA Cup fifth round, by now very used to playing men's football. Being a part of a historic football club was a dream come true for me. They were, and are, a massive club up there with the best. To be part of a club of that stature made me hugely proud. To think that when I arrived as a fourteen-year-old, I was met and looked after by my great friend Gary Speed. I will never forget his friendship. My heroes, like Gary McAllister the midfield legend, and David Batty, who I looked up to as a role model, were there. I watched them training, learnt from the best and was inspired by them. It was a club in the Champions League, the UEFA Cup and playing in the Premier League every week.

I played for Wales in every age group and I captained every side I played in as well. I also played for the Wales B team. In a friendly against Switzerland for the under 21s, Mark Hughes approached me at half time and asked me to come off. Straight away I wondered what I'd done wrong but instead he invited me to be part of the senior squad the next day. It was fantastic – I couldn't sleep at all! I just kept repeating, 'I'm in the squad! I'm in the squad!' but I couldn't believe I'd get on the field. I made my debut for Wales at eighteen years of age, coming on for Gary Speed in the second half. It was such a proud moment for me to play alongside Chris Coleman, Mark Pembridge, John Hartson and Andy Melville. I can't remember many of the details because the experience itself was so wonderful. I was on cloud nine!

I made my full Welsh debut against Qatar. To start a game is so much more satisfying than coming off the bench. You get the chance to stand there, to sing the anthem and feel that you're right at the centre of things. I clutched my heart and cried. We won 1-0. The boys joked that not many players can say they made their debut when Wales won the game!

All in all, I had thirteen senior caps over a five-year

period. I had the good fortune to play against major sides like Brazil and Portugal. Lining up in a packed Millennium Stadium, Cardiff, with 74,000 people all singing the anthem, is a moment that I will never forget.

I moved from Leeds to Leicester for a transfer fee of three and a half million pounds, at the age of twenty. That was a fortune at the time. Other clubs had bid for me too. But Robbie Savage encouraged me to join him and Muzzy Izzet there. To fill Neil Lennon's boots was a massive challenge and to take on the number 7 shirt that he'd worn was a real inspiration for me. Like Leeds, Leicester as a club had a great family environment. I was made to feel very welcome which was important to me. I was young and desperate to play. My first game for the club was against Charlton, then we played West Ham and I was awarded 'Man of the Match' in both games. I felt proud and quickly at home at Leicester.

Sadly, my career was stopped short by injury. First of all, I ruptured my cruciate, a common knee injury in football. I was out for a year as I had to have knee reconstruction. During that time, the club was relegated. It was hard playing at a different level in the Championship. Then I was taken on loan to Notts Forest, and playing Ajax in a pre-season friendly, my leg was trapped underneath me, causing my back to twist badly. The result was two prolapsed discs. I was rushed to hospital and spent four months bed-bound.

I now had to face an injury that was very uncommon in football. This was more of a rugby injury. I had nerve problems and couldn't move. The surgeon told me before the operation that he didn't think I'd play football again. My first thought was that I needed to be able to walk again. I felt angry because lots of people were giving up on me. Everyone was so negative. I didn't know anyone in football who'd had this type of injury and got through it. I had no one to talk to, no one to give me hope and inspiration. Having to tell the media and everyone else that I was officially retiring from the game was very hard. It was the end of my career. I disguised my sadness for the sake of others. Football was everything to me.

Thankfully, other opportunities came my way and I took up broadcasting for the BBC and Sky TV. To change completely from being a player to an observer was hard to come to terms with at first but, with great support from family and friends, I managed to adapt to my new life. I was reminded to concentrate on what I had, not what I didn't have. That positive mindset has kept me going and improved my physical fitness. I went from being barely able to walk to running marathons. It's all in the mind ...

My life has constantly been meeting challenges, setting goals, reaching targets and telling myself, 'I can do that.' It's funny that I had no problem playing in front of thousands of spectators, but standing up and speaking in front of a hundred or so people really worries me! It's out of my comfort zone but I prepare carefully, speak from the heart, and do my best.

My new role in Swansea Football Club is Lead under 16 academy coach. I joined the club as a part-time coach, asked to pass on my experiences to younger players. My role as a player was as a midfielder but as a coach now, I have to know the role of the goalkeeper, defender, midfielder and striker, as well as having the necessary people skills to motivate all my teams.

All the things I've learnt along the way are helping me now. I'm still very enthusiastic. I still love the beautiful game. I want to give back to the younger generation some of the joy I've experienced.

CHAPTER SIX

Josh Navidi

Rugby player. Cardiff Blues, Wales.

I won my first international rugby cap for Wales playing against Japan in 2013. It was a memorable match for many reasons. Wales lost 23-8 to the Cherry Blossoms, coached then by Eddie Jones, and I was knocked out and broke my nose! Not a great start to an international career.

My dad Hedy is from Iran and he did a lot of wrestling which is a huge sport in that country. He came to Wales when he was eighteen to study Civil Engineering at Bangor University, and it was there at a local disco he met my mum Euros who is from Anglesey. He speaks Farsi, Mum speaks Welsh – two great cultures coming together.

Dad used to be the Welsh national wrestling coach and once took a GB wrestling team training session. The result was that he made them all sick and they never came back! He's taken me for a few sessions and, to be honest, wrestling training is far tougher than anything else I've done! I'd rather stick to rugby any day!

Dad is a very honest person. After a game, although his rugby knowledge is not that good, he knows instinctively how well or how badly I've played. I appreciate that very much. He's always said to me, 'Every game could be your last', and that's how I've always played. I go out there on the pitch and I give it my all.

I went to Brynteg School in Bridgend, where we lived. Academic studies didn't come easily to me, but I was inspired, as was my brother Sam, by my parents' work ethic. I wasn't one of those people who could just turn up for an exam without revising. I had to make time to sit down and learn what I'd been taught if I wanted to achieve good results. I would revise, take a break and then return to the books again. My mum and dad constantly reminded me of the value of studying and having a good education and sometimes even bribed me to study – although there weren't huge sums of money involved! I was, however, good at sport and with the guidance of teacher and coach Richard Harris our team got to two school rugby finals. Brynteg has a fine rugby tradition and former pupils include Dr Jack Matthews, JPR Williams, Gavin Henson and Rob Howley.

Luckily, I've always thought 'Get out there and get on with it' if things aren't going too well. My dad's positive influence has been good for me. I get my mental attitude from him. I really admired the way he worked and the way he trained. When I got the bus for school at 7.30am in the morning, I'd see my dad out training for the marathon. He'd probably already been running for an hour, but he'd still be there driving himself on. You couldn't miss him because he had bright blue gloves on! He's always just got up and got on with things in his life. He believes you've got to do things for yourself – no one else can do them for you – and he's taught me that.

At sixteen, two things happened which were to have a huge impact on me. My dad was quite keen on taking me to New Zealand to improve my rugby education and, as luck would have it, my hero, the late, great All Blacks legend, Jonah Lomu, came to Bridgend. After a question and answer session in the rugby club, he talked to my dad and me for about three quarters of an hour. I listened, mesmerised, as the big man talked about New Zealand and its rugby traditions and said it was absolutely the best place to go. So, two days after my last GCSEs had finished, Dad and I flew to Canterbury, New Zealand. I was to attend the famous St Bede's College, which had a special programme that combined formal education with rugby training and playing. Although passionate and successful in rugby terms, the college always stressed the need to have 'something to fall back on' when a rugby-playing career was over.

I couldn't get over how important rugby was in New Zealand. No matter who you met, they knew all about the All Blacks and they were so proud of their sport and their team. If a game was on, the streets were empty – everyone would be watching! It was the same at St Bede's. If we were playing on a Saturday it would be in front of a packed crowd all there to support us. Coaches from Canterbury and members of the All Blacks team would come in and speak to us after the game, taking time to talk to us about what they'd seen. It was good for us as youngsters to be given advice from the very best.

The work ethic in rugby was immense and I learnt a lot from that. Each boy in the team supported each other on the pitch. If you looked to your left or your right, they would be there and would die for you out there on that field. Their mental attitude was so strong. It didn't matter who you were playing, they always believed that they were better than the opposition. When they ran onto the field, they weren't worried about anything, other than giving the best performance they could.

Although learning about rugby in a different country was quite daunting, I was more nervous about learning the Haka than anything else. Every player has to learn their Haka and you spend time after training going through it together. Every school has a different Haka and it's a matter of huge pride. I didn't want to get it wrong!

After two years in New Zealand, I was offered a place at Canterbury Academy. It was very tempting but, deep down, Dad and I knew it was time to return home. He had businesses in Wales and I was a Welsh lad who above all dreamt of playing for my country. When we came back, I worked full time for my dad in his gym and then had a trial period with the Cardiff Blues Academy. I was given sprint tests and weights tests and was told what a future with the club might be like. We used to train in the morning at the academy and then play for one of the Blues' regional club teams. Mine was Glamorgan Wanderers on the outskirts of Cardiff. My coach there was Richard Hodges who then joined the academy and is now with the Blues. I have always been pleased to have his constructive feedback after playing in a game.

I was fortunate to captain a successful Wales under 20 side and then came my senior debut against Leinster, away, where I came off the bench. The following week we played against Gloucester. I faced Brian O'Driscoll in the first game and then Carlos Spencer in the second, both heroes of mine who I'd grown up watching on TV and looked up to. And now I was on the same pitch as them! Some of the Blues players, too, such as Gareth Thomas and Gareth Williams had trained in my dad's gym. I'd watched them as a young boy and been in awe of them. Now we were all playing in the same team!

I don't get nervous before games. I never look too far ahead. I always have an end goal in the back of my mind, of course, but I just think for each game, I've got to give my best and hope to keep progressing that way.

In 2013, I was chosen to be a member of the successful

Six Nations squad but didn't get to play. A couple of months after the championship was over, Alan Phillips, the team manager, handed me a box and in it was a medal as a squad member. At the time I was shocked because I hadn't played in any of the games, but then I realised how important it was as recognition of what being part of a squad means. I appreciate now how every member of that squad contributes in some way, whether they're selected for games or not. Every person plays their part. It's easy to get downhearted if you don't get selected, but I've always taken the attitude that you just play your best rugby for your club and, if you do that week in week out, you'll get the chance to wear that red jersey. I've always said that I've got to play well for the Blues before I can even be considered to play for Wales.

As teammates in the Blues, we push each other to give our best. Competition for places is healthy because it's for the good of the team. It makes us train harder and play better. It's no good sitting and moaning, 'Why am I not being selected?' You've just got to get on with it and prove, through your training and your skills, that you deserve a place in the team. My mum keeps the 'Man of the Match' and 'Player of the Season' awards that I've been given, and my Grogg statue has pride of place. I only found out on Twitter that it had been made and I managed to get one for my parents and one for my brother. Richard Hughes, who makes them at his world-famous shop in Pontypridd, found mine quite difficult because of my dreadlocks. I'd added blonde bits into my hair when I met him and he was gutted, but I thought it looked amazing! I told him not to worry. He's done such a fantastic job on all the players – the Groggs have become real collector's items!

Now I really enjoy working with Apollo Teaching Services, going into schools to encourage children to get more involved with sport. I enjoy coaching in one session and then following it up by going to see pupils play and see how I've made a difference. It's good to see the change in the way that they cope with things and how they respond to what you tell them. It's great to be able to support children with their sport and show them how they can transfer the skills they learn in sport into skills for life. My dad was such a positive role model for me and I'd like to think that I can do the same for others. Physical fitness is so important now, as is developing the right attitude to training and playing, and conducting yourself properly both on and off the field.

Jonah Lomu explained to me when I was a young schoolboy that no matter what happens on the rugby field, you meet up with your opponents afterwards in the club house as friends. It's not all about winning and losing, though winning is obviously important. If you win, you celebrate as a team. If you lose, you pick yourself up as a team too. My hero was right. Some sports might have a different view of things but in rugby that's what's important.

CHAPTER SEVEN

Nathan Stephens

Sledge hockey player and athlete. GB Sledge
Hockey team, Team Wales Commonwealth Games,
World Champion, Team GB Paralympic Games.

Like many Welsh youngsters, I often dreamt of playing sport for my country. I was a good defender and goalkeeper in football and my grandad had high hopes that I would be a great Welsh prop when I grew up.

I loved being outside and my friends and I used to play by the railway tracks. On my ninth birthday, I decided to jump on the ladders of a passing slow freight train. That's about the last thing I remember as my foot slipped, and I was dragged under the train. My brother, friend and cousin got me off the track and went for help. A kind lady gave me drinks, in between my slipping in and out of consciousness. One leg had gone, the other was in a very bad way. I wasn't very happy when the fire brigade cut off my new Manchester United shirt but cheered up when a helicopter air ambulance airlifted me to hospital. What a day, what a birthday! In every sense it was going to change my life completely.

From that moment on, I had to think, 'Where am I going to go? What am I going to do?' Trying to get over that has always been about not letting disability *become* me and dictate who I am. I've always been determined to take over the disability and just get on with my life. I've always tried to live that life thinking that no matter how many disappointments come along, there's always a way to overcome them.

I developed that determination and positive attitude whilst I was growing up and I quickly realised that sport was going to be a big part of all that I did. Thanks in no small way to the fantastic support of my family, friends and teachers, I played rugby and football in my own way, enjoyed swimming and even became a GB International at ice sledge hockey! Then, at the Newport Rotary Games, I was spotted by Anthony Hughes, who became my coach, and encouraged me to have a go at athletics. There and then, I knew this was something I really wanted to do and be successful doing it. I made the very tough decision to give up ice sledge hockey and concentrate on athletics. I desperately wanted to win medals and emulate my Welsh sporting heroes. But life is far from simple, and even though I was achieving success and enjoying my new field events of shot, discus and javelin, there were to be many highs and lows along the way.

Probably the first major disappointment I had to overcome was when I injured my shoulder just after the Beijing Paralympics in 2009. I wasn't aware at first just how bad the shoulder injury was and what was the extent of the damage that I would need to contend with. I had to go for surgery knowing that the World Championships were not too far away. I had to take a full year out of training, then focus on getting myself back on track, all the time knowing how hard my fellow competitors had been working and improving whilst I was out of the sport. It was hard lying in my hospital bed in London, all on my own, far away from friends and family. Once again in my life, it all seemed too much.

Luckily my physio at the time, Lily, was there for me. She was my rock, my support. Every morning we'd do the same routine, exactly the same things, until there was a clear pattern and structure for me to follow. I'd felt so abandoned, and it took me right back to being nine years old again in a hospital bed, alone and scared. She made me see that the only person who could get me out of this dark place was me. It's good to get things out in the open and it's good to say how you feel, but in the end it doesn't matter who you talk to or how many people you tell about your fears, the final answer has to come from you. You start to answer your own questions and begin to trust yourself. This makes you realise that there is always a way forward.

I told myself that this was a time for me to start from scratch and to work on the areas I was weak at. Okay, so

I couldn't work on my shoulder, but I knew I needed to improve my core strength and work on power for my left-hand side, so the answer was there for me. We did that programme for six to eight months, day in, day out. It was my focus, my new goal: to get back to where I wanted to be.

My first javelin competition after that was in Crystal Palace. After six months out of the sport, I threw a personal best with my first throw. By resetting my goal, the time off had allowed me to grow and develop, to work on my weaknesses and come back stronger! It gave me time to realise who I was and what I could be as an athlete and as a person. That throw also qualified me for the World Championships in 2011 in New Zealand. However, I felt unprepared for this, mentally, as well as physically, because I hadn't completed the number of throws that I wanted to in order to be in the best condition. I made myself think back to the time with Lily and I told myself that it had worked before and it would work again, if I talked myself through my fears and trusted in my own voice. I said to myself quietly, 'It only takes one throw to win it.' It worked. I sat in front of the mirror with my coach Anthony and just visualised a lot of different throws and different techniques, working quietly towards the goal that I had set myself. I went to the pool regularly, keeping myself fit and active, all the time building trust in myself.

The only throwing training session I had in New Zealand nearly went terribly wrong. It was pouring down with rain, I was completely stressed and angry, and had a real toddler tantrum, staying out in the rain with my coach beside me. The head coach came out and said, 'He needs to come in. He's going to get a dreadful cold out there. Get him in!' But Anthony knew me better and said, 'No! He needs to do this for himself. He knows that.' I got out my throwing frame, sat in my wheelchair, picked up my javelin and just launched it … and it was the furthest I've ever thrown! It's actually the furthest throw to this day, too! I looked up and said, 'Right, okay, that's me done.' And it was the last throw before my competition.

I've carried that mentality ever since. Pick yourself back up. You've just got to get out there and do it. I tell myself, 'You know what you need to do. You know how to throw – just relax and get on with it.' It's simple but it worked.

I came back from New Zealand as World Champion and went on later that year to break the world record. 2011 was the highest point of my career after 2010 being the worst possible – but of course that wasn't the end of it! 2012 was on the horizon … a home Paralympic Games in London! The buzz was amazing, and I couldn't wait to get ready for it. I went into training too hard, too soon and my shoulder was injured again. I told myself, 'You've done

67

this before. You can do it again,' all the time knowing that the biggest competition of my life was coming closer. I repeated all the rehab, luckily with my wife, Charlene, and family around me this time. They were wonderful as always and did everything they could to support me.

Sadly London 2012 didn't go so well and this time it was a lot harder to take. I had gone in thinking this would be my Games and that I could achieve a paralympic medal. I was there as World Champion and world record holder, but it didn't go the way I planned due to a rule change and my previous success counted for nothing. My family were devastated, and the result of the competition hurt them. They wanted it for me probably more than I wanted it for myself. Seeing the looks on their faces when I first opened my eyes took me back to being nine years old lying in that hospital bed. It was hard, painful and horrific. I came back from London 2012 in a very dark place, not knowing if I wanted to continue in my sport or even in any sport. In my mind, I'd done nothing wrong, and that rule change was for me an injustice in front of the eyes of the world. But I kept myself together, determined not to be sour or bitter. It took me a good few months to pick myself up, but I knew I'd been through worse things in my life and that I would get over it and carry on. I knew that it was just another setback I'd have to overcome. It was only me who could do that. On the positive side, I could still say that I had been selected for Team GB.

I didn't want to end my career on a sour note. I told myself, 'It's sport – things happen.' I couldn't let one decision affect who I am and what I am. I changed my focus, picked myself back up again and trained for the European Championships in Swansea. Once again, though, the rules for the classification of athletes were changed. It would have been easy for me to feel despondent once more but I wouldn't let this beat me. My coach and I changed my throwing frame and my technique and I gave it one last blast in Swansea. Unfortunately, that didn't work out either. I was left with some hard questions for myself: 'Why did I start sport in the first place? What does it mean to me?' I decided I wasn't enjoying it and stepped away from it. I felt it was turning me into someone I didn't want to be.

So I decided to work on my career and, as part of that, to work with younger athletes and help them avoid some of the things that I had been through. I wanted to help them to be more resilient, more able to deal with the highs – and the lows – of sport. I wanted to talk to them about the importance of working with success and – more importantly – of coping when things don't go as planned. The athletes I work with have horrific injuries and illnesses. Working with 'Help for Heroes' has highlighted how people deal with huge suffering and refuse to be deterred. I hope to make a difference to the lives of others. I've had a fantastic career that has taken me to some amazing places where I've met some equally amazing people. I decided to channel my energy and focus into this, and working with Disability Sport Wales has helped me to do that.

But there was still a nagging doubt which my wife picked up on. She said, 'You're not yourself. You need to find something for you.' Now she might well have been suggesting I take up something as a hobby – but I went at it with my usual determination! I tried kayaking and people told me I was really good. Also, at the time I was working with Welsh Weightlifting on their performance pathways and they said, 'Ever tried powerlifting before?' Well, I'd been to the gym before a few times (!) so I thought: I'll give it a go; after all, my wife says I ought to do something for me! It would keep me active, so why not give it a go?

I took part in a powerlifting competition in Hungary and it was then suggested that I compete in the Commonwealth Games at the Gold Coast, Australia. After all, I'd made the rankings and I was on the list to be in the team! I'd never taken part in the Commonwealth Games before and this was my chance! I told my wife and her response was, 'I thought you were just doing this as a hobby!' She was, and has always been, one hundred per cent behind every decision I'd ever made but she had also seen that sport, which had given me so much, had also nearly destroyed me. She was tentative and nervous in case it went wrong and hurt me again. But she had seen me build myself back up and regain my confidence after the Paralympic Games in London and, as ever, was on my side. She said, 'You're great now. Don't let sport control you. You control sport if that's what you want.' It would be a final opportunity to show those who had destroyed my dreams at one point in my life that they had not destroyed me.

I did go to the Commonwealth Games. I finished last – but I absolutely loved it! It was the first time I'd been able to put on a Welsh vest for my country, as opposed to the GB vest I'd worn many times before. I'm a proud Welshman and to compete under a Welsh flag was an honour that filled me with pride. It was amazing! It was hard being away from my wife and my family again, but they understood I needed to do this. I returned home, and she looked at me and said, 'You're yourself again. Is that it now? Are you done?'

Actually, Birmingham 2022 is another home Games ... It could be my very last one and that's what I'm aiming for now. It's been a tough road, but I realise why I do sport. As an elite athlete you live in a bubble but you need to prepare yourself for the highs and lows. You have to manage the good times and the bad, as in life. I could have stopped at any point when things were against me.

You have to find out what's really important to you. I've refused to be bitter when things have gone against me and decisions have been made that aren't fair in my eyes.

When I stopped competing, I set new goals for myself. I had to ask myself some tough questions about what skills I had for life and work after sport – I'd never even written a CV. My new ambitions included learning how to dance and I appeared on a special edition of *Strictly Come Dancing*. That was very different but I had a great time!

Life is never straightforward, and you can take a detour, take a rest and set off again. The people around you are important. Listen to those you trust and those who want the best for you and listen to yourself. Hold onto the positive!

CHAPTER EIGHT
Anna Hursey

Table tennis player. Team Wales, Commonwealth Games.

I am the youngest person ever to represent Wales at senior level in any sport ... I was ten years old at the time.

I'd tried gymnastics and swimming, but when I started playing table tennis at the age of five, I really liked it and knew it was the sport for me. I used to play against my dad, Larry, and in the early days he usually won. But finally, at the age of seven, I beat him and he hasn't beaten me since!

My parents knew from that early age that I had a real talent for this sport. My mother, Xiuli Zhang, was born in China and she is aware of how highly table tennis is regarded in Asia. My parents met in China and then moved to Wales where my dad's family lived and where I was born. It was difficult to find anyone to coach me as I was so young, so my mum took six weeks' unpaid leave from her job and went with me to China to train and be coached. I could hardly see over the table, but I was very determined! The coaches were impressed, and my mum tells me that I was playing alongside a six-year-old Chinese boy and the coaches told him to look at me as I was good! It was an amazing time – we were constantly practising, and

I learnt so much. Each day there was an hour of intensive coaching which really improved my technique. After the sessions, I stayed to play with the other children and that was great fun. I'm fluent in both Chinese and English so it was no problem to be coached there.

My dad helped me at the beginning, but he wasn't a trained technical coach and he wanted the best for me. So when we returned from China, I continued to train at the Penlan Leisure Centre in Swansea with Betty Gray and Roy Towell. Then I was spotted by the national coaches in Wales. Aled Howell had represented Wales as a player and his expertise helped me so much. He and Andrew Jones from Mumbles encouraged me and made me feel so positive. I regularly beat adult players which can't have been very nice for them. In fact, some got quite cross after they lost!

When I was six, I won my first Welsh national title and I remember proudly holding my trophy in two hands and smiling for the camera. I began training with the Cardiff City Table Tennis Club as this was open all week and I would have more time to try out all my new skills. Nathan Thomas, the club's director, really helped me. He understands me and can always bring out the best in me as a player and as a person. He can sort any problems and gets me playing well straight away because I trust him. He knows how to build me up and how to calm me down. I can go to talk to him when I've been successful and also when things haven't gone so well. My parents moved to Cardiff to be closer to the club as they could see this would allow me to reach my full potential. They have been so supportive, always trying to do the best for me.

At nine years of age, I went to live in Harbin in China for a year with my mum, to improve my table tennis and to go to school there. She realised that to be the best, I had to train with the best. Although I missed my dad very much during that time, I made lots of new friends. I marched every day in school and, like all the other pupils, had to salute the flag. I trained for eight hours each day, six days a week. It was very hard, but my game improved a lot. China is the leading country in the world for table tennis and is the best place to learn how to play. It has won twenty-eight out of the thirty-two Olympic gold medals in the sport. The Chinese say that table tennis is like chess played at a hundred miles an hour. It's a thinking game. You have to concentrate all the time when you're at the table. Every single ball that you play, you're thinking about spin and power. You use your brain and you use your whole body.

Sometimes when you're playing it's hard to keep focused, because opponents, coaches and the crowd watching will try anything to put you off your game. The spectators will clap and cheer for their favourites and make a lot of noise. Coaches might make faces at you before the match starts to try and scare you. You have to be mentally strong in this sport. When people do that, I just ignore it and try not to worry. My parents and coaches always tell me that it really isn't important if your opponent has more supporters in the crowd than you. It might affect you a little, but you just get on with it.

My mother often reminds me of a time when I was playing a girl from China in her home town. She was two years older than me and had a lot of loud support amongst the spectators. It got to me and I was losing badly, two sets to nil behind and 9-2 down in the third set. I was playing well but I felt everything was against me and there were tears in my eyes. A teammate who had finished her game early came over to support and encourage every shot I played. I slowly clawed my way back. As I began to win more points, the crowd started reacting too and started to cheer for me. I eventually won the match and I won the crowd over as well! It was a great feeling and after that victory I became quite well known in China. When I came back home, I had a back injury, maybe as a result of all the training and playing that I'd done. The physiotherapist told me I had to strengthen my core muscles which I did, and my back got better.

My playing had certainly improved after all the coaching and hard work. At the age of ten I was chosen by the Welsh selectors to make my first senior international appearance for my country against Kosovo in a European qualifying match. I was understandably very nervous before my match at the National Sports Centre in Cardiff, but I won my match 3-0 and, very importantly, Wales won 3-0 overall. Winning in my first international was amazing!

I love competing and making new friends in other countries, but I do miss the friends I have at home. I know that special friends who are close to me have said, 'We miss Anna. She's away a lot and I don't get to see her that much.' Although a great deal of my time is taken up with training and playing, I do like to relax, chill out to music and have a sleepover with my friends. Although difficult, it's important to try to balance my dedication to table tennis with normal everyday life. I usually am quite nervous before a match and, as part of my preparation, I always paint my nails – mostly red. Red nails for Wales! It makes me feel better and ready to play.

Last year I was selected to represent Wales in the Commonwealth Games in Australia, at eleven years of age – the youngest competitor there. I was given lots of good luck messages and banners of support and that really cheered me. I couldn't believe the number of people at the opening ceremony, a huge colourful gathering of competitors and spectators. Apparently, I was mentioned in the stadium, but it was so loud there I couldn't hear anything! I took loads of photographs though and I'll never forget being there. The fact that I was so young meant I attracted a huge amount of media interest. I was allocated a bodyguard and provided with a car for me and the team in case things got out of hand.

The first match was doubles against India, the number one seeds. I was again very nervous but my partner, Charlotte, helped and encouraged me and after a close match we managed to win. India's doubles team went on to win the gold medal so our performance in beating two members of that team was very good. I lost in the second round of the singles after winning my first match in straight sets and our team got knocked out in the quarter final, losing to hosts Australia 3-1. The Games were fantastic!

Looking to the future, my ambition is to one day compete in the Olympic Games. Whether I get selected for 2020 in Tokyo, I'm not so sure, as I'll still only be fourteen years old. But I am determined to do everything I can to get to the Paris Olympics in 2024, and I want to win a medal! I have been very lucky to have the help and guidance of Team Anna, my mum and dad, brother Mark, Wales national team coaches Ryan and Stephen Jenkins, my local coach Nathan Thomas and my friends throughout the years. I still train very hard and my Chinese coach Jiawang (Leo) has come to live in our house. We practise together in a special table tennis room that my parents have had built in our garden.

Although sometimes I don't feel like training or playing, I tell myself it'll all be worth it in the end. It's been a rollercoaster time for me, with lots of interviews, my own website, YouTube clips and several appearances on television with celebrities like Jamie Redknapp and James Corden. Also, being shortlisted for BBC Young Sports Personality of the Year was unbelievable! Last year alone, I travelled to ten different countries. In many ways, that was great and very exciting but what I missed more than anything during all that travel was my own bed!

CHAPTER NINE
Lynn Davies CBE

Athlete. Olympic, European and
Commonwealth gold medallist.

It was wet, windy and miserable on that October day in Tokyo in 1964. I was in the final of the long jump competition at the Olympic Games up against a Russian and an American athlete. They were the best in the world at that time, so my realistic hope was that I would win a bronze medal.

In my mind, I went back to Wales and the long jump pit at Cardiff Training College. There, in mid-winter, in wet and windy conditions such as those in Tokyo, I'd jumped eight metres. If I did this now, maybe, just maybe, I could win ... gold!

My interest in sport had been first kindled when I attended Ogmore Grammar School in Bridgend. In winter I enjoyed rugby and football, played on the wing for my school rugby team and had trials for Cardiff City. In summer we did athletics and my favourite competitions were sprinting and jumping. At a Welsh Athletics meeting in 1961, I won the triple jump in a new Welsh record and came second in the long jump.

It was there that I met Ron Pickering and it was there

that we forged a coach-athlete relationship that was to bring us great success in years to come. There is no comparison between then and now. Nowadays top athletes have back-up teams full of coaches, doctors, physios, nutritionists and psychologists. Back in my day, I had Ron and his wife Jean. Ron was my coach, mentor, medic and psychologist. A hard taskmaster, he set tough goals for me, but I was happy to do the hard work because I soon realised that was the only way to achieve success. My nutritionist was Ron's wife Jean because she was a great cook and prepared all the 'right' foods for me! I did go to see a physiotherapist from time to time, Gerry Lewis from Newport, who also looked after, and was much loved by, the Welsh rugby team. Gerry was a great character. He was always upbeat, a great personality and very positive – he lifted your spirits.

I moved from Nantymoel, my home, to be a student at Cardiff Training College with all its excellent facilities. Ron Pickering moved from London to Cardiff to work with me. We set our goals – to make me the very best athlete that I could be. At the age of twenty, I narrowly missed out on the bronze medal for long jump at the Commonwealth Games in Perth but it gave me a taste for international success.

When I was selected for the Olympic Games two years later in Tokyo, I just about qualified for the final having had two 'no jumps'. My main rivals were Igor Ter-Ovanesyan from Russia who had won bronze in the previous two

Olympics and defending champion and world record holder Ralph Boston from America. He had won gold in Rome four years earlier and as a young schoolboy I'd watched him do that on television. They were both superb athletes and clearly favourites to win the competition. However, two days prior to the final I was sitting in the café in the Olympic Village when Mary Rand came in to show us the gold medal she'd won in the women's long jump. That really was great motivation for me to do well!

There were no great expectations for me, except perhaps at best a bronze medal, but because I'd trained so hard in similar awful weather conditions at home, I felt that I could turn this to my advantage. I looked up at the flags at the top of the stadium which were swirling around in the wind and the rain. I waited for the wind to drop and raced down the runway. Immediately I knew I'd jumped a long distance. It took what seemed an age to measure but then the scoreboard swung around and showed 8.07 metres, which put me in gold medal position. Last up were my two main rivals. Boston's jump was greeted with a huge roar from the crowd but the scoreboard showed 8.03 metres, so I still led by four centimetres. Last to go was the Russian. 8.07 metres was well within his reach, but he fell short. His jump was only 7.99 metres. The gold medal was mine and I'm still Wales' first and only individual Olympic athletics champion! The favourites had been beaten. It's a good lesson: never underestimate what might happen in sport and in life. Sometimes there are surprises and, through hard work and dedication, the underdog can win. You have one chance every four years as an athlete at the Olympic Games so you have to give it your best.

The celebrations when I came home were amazing. When I got off the train in London there was a great big banner across Paddington Station saying, 'Welcome Home, Lynn.' When I arrived at Cardiff railway station there must have been 2,500 people outside and I had to get on a porter's trolley with the Mayor of Cardiff and make a speech. I thought this kind of welcome home was only reserved for The Beatles! On the journey from Cardiff up to Nantymoel, we had to go up through all the little villages – Ogmore Vale, Blackmill, Bryncethin – and all the way up people were lining the roads and children were waving flags having been given the day off school. They'd put bunting and flags across every street – it was incredible, amazing. I had gone to the Olympics just beginning to get noticed as quite a good athlete in the British team, but I came back with an Olympic gold medal. In those days we didn't win many of those, so it was very special. They even marked out 8.07 metres on the pavement outside my home in Nantymoel!

Now for the first time in my life, I had a full-time job,

teaching. I switched from being a PE student and Olympic athlete to becoming a geography and PE teacher in Bridgend Grammar School. That kept me very grounded and of course we were all amateurs in those days. You weren't allowed to make money from athletics – if you did that you would be disqualified from competing. I was only coming up to twenty-two so I had achieved success at a very young age, but with Ron's help there was more to come. I managed to win gold in a Welsh vest in the Commonwealth Games in Kingston, Jamaica in 1966 and two months later won gold in the European championships in Budapest. I was the first British athlete to be the reigning Olympic, European and Commonwealth champion – the next man to do that was Daley Thompson, so it was an elite club to be in.

Winning was great but what I enjoyed most was the lifestyle – I enjoyed training and competing and the fact that I won was a great bonus. To be able to go to Tokyo, Jamaica and then all over Europe and America, all expenses paid, was a huge luxury back then, though it was hard to hold down a teaching job and compete. I competed in three Olympic Games – Tokyo, Mexico and Munich – over a twelve-year period. Looking back, it was a very happy and satisfying time.

Obviously, times have changed since then and things have moved on. The biggest difference I think has been in the last twenty years. In Atlanta in 1996 rower Steve Redgrave won one Olympic gold medal. In London 2012 we won sixty-five medals and thirty-two golds. I think the main reason for that improvement is Lottery funding. In my day we were amateurs with full-time jobs competing against the Russians and the Americans. The Russians were state-sponsored, and the American athletes had scholarships in universities; they were virtually professionals.

In order to win or succeed in anything, the qualities you need are talent, desire, commitment and perseverance. I finished fourth in my first Commonwealth Games and ninth in my first European Championships. These were poor results the year before the Tokyo Olympics but my desire, commitment, perseverance and tenacity leading up to Tokyo, and my self-belief to stay the course paid off. Nobody expected me to win. Realistically my aim was to perform well but preparation, persistence and a little bit of good luck got me the gold. Preparation is the key.

The most important step in achieving anything in life is setting specific goals to get your mind focused. You have to work out what you want, work out what you have to do to get it, and be prepared to pay the price and make the sacrifices. It's about setting clear goals for yourself and being responsible for achieving them. My motto has always been, 'If it's to be, it's up to me.' Of course, it does help to have somebody working with you to achieve these goals – a teacher, parent, friend or coach. In athletics, I set my goals with Ron Pickering and we used to monitor and discuss progress. It also helps to write them down and keep a record. Your goals can change from one year to the next and as you get better and achieve your goals, you need to set new ones to challenge yourself.

We know a lot more about goal-setting now than we did then. Basically, there are three types of goals – for example, in athletics you have an outcome goal. This will be to win a race, or to gain second or third – and it's a strong motivator but it's not within your control. You cannot control your opponent's performance, only yours. It's a goal, but it's not the most important one. The second one is a performance goal. You set yourself times and distances so, for example, you might want to say: my goal today is to run 200m in twenty-four seconds, or long jump six metres. These goals are in your control if they are realistic. The last, and most important, is the process goal, where you focus on technique, such as a good start, and strong finish in a sprint, or your run-up, take-off, flight or landing in long jump. If you achieve these process goals, you're likely to be successful. There's no more you could have done.

In an international career of eleven years, I've competed in thirteen major games, winning seven long jump medals, setting seventeen British and Commonwealth records, twenty-five Welsh records and winning six AAA (British) and eight Welsh titles. Not a bad effort! It wasn't all plain sailing – you can't win all the time and it's how you deal with both winning and losing that's important. But it's very satisfying to look back to see what you have achieved and how the hard work and goal-setting paid off. It really helps to develop your mental attitude and gives you the motivation to achieve something that is important to you.

I've been very fortunate in that, after retiring from athletics, I've kept in close contact with the sport I love. My career took me to Canada as Track and Field Director, I worked for the Sports Council for Wales, I've been team manager of the British team in two Olympic Games and President of UK Athletics. I think that the lessons learnt in sport are good life lessons. Many sportsmen and women are very good role models. Their experience and success help to inspire future generations. In today's society lots of people want success immediately and they're not prepared to put in the hard work and practice and dedication – but it's a long-term thing. A sports person's career can last anything from five years to fifteen years, so you have to stick at it. In order to be good at anything – work, music or sport – you have to put in the hours, so it does need a lot of focus and application.

Build a good team around you, people whose advice

you trust, who want the best for you and will help you along the way. Have your dreams but know you will have to work hard. It won't be instant celebrity full of fame and fortune, but the long-term success you might achieve will be well worth the effort.

Congratulations on completing
a 2019 Quick Read.

The Quick Reads project, with bite-sized books, is designed to get readers back into the swing of reading, and reading for pleasure. So we sincerely hope you enjoyed this book.

Got an opinion?

Your feedback can make this project better. Now you've read one of the Quick Reads series visit www.readingwales.org.uk or Twitter @quickreads2019 to post your feedback.

→ Why did you choose this book?

→ What did you like about it?

→ What do you think of the Quick Reads series?

→ Which Quick Reads would you like to see in the future?

What next?

Now that you've finished one Quick Read – got time for another? Look out for the other title in the 2019 Quick Reads series – *Music to Make Friends By* by Hayley Long.

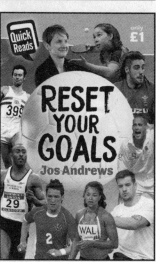

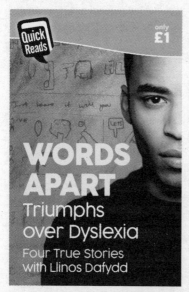

only **£1**

WORDS APART

Triumphs over Dyslexia

Four True Stories
with Llinos Dafydd

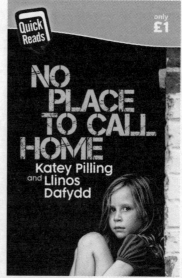

only **£1**

NO PLACE TO CALL HOME

Katey Pilling
and Llinos
Dafydd

only **£1**

Music to Make Friends By

a life loving pop music

by Hayley Long

only **£1**

RESET YOUR GOALS

Jos Andrews

Jos Andrews

Jos is based in Cardiff and currently works as a freelance writer, producer and consultant on a number of projects. In addition, she is a project manager and trainer, and her clients include Wales TUC and their Wales Union Fund Partners, the Open University, Digital Communities Wales, The Fostering Network and a range of private companies. Jos also has particular interest in working on projects featuring sport, education and human interest.

Jos is a former BBC producer, creative writer and consultant with extensive experience in the media, education, training, arts and public relations.

She has thirteen years' experience in the BBC as a television, radio and online producer in the Department of Education and Learning, with a varied and diverse work portfolio working as a series producer at two Olympic and Paralympic Games, Commonwealth Games, European and World Championships and Six Nations rugby.

Jos also has a background in teaching in schools and in further and higher education institutions, as well as being an examiner with projects focused on engagement and learning by stealth.

Her career highlights include co-authoring seven Quick Reads books for the Welsh Books Council, writing, developing and producing an eight-year multiplatform educational series for the BBC, and being honoured as a torchbearer at the London 2012 Olympics, nominated for work in inspiring young people.

RILY

rily.co.uk